Real-World STEM: Develop Economical Solar Power

Real-World STEM:
Develop Economical
Solar Power

Stuart A. Kallen

ReferencePoint
Press®

San Diego, CA

LIBRARY OF CONGRESS CATALOGING-IN-PUBLICATION DATA

Name: Kallen, Stuart A., 1955– author.
Title: Real-World STEM: Develop Economical Solar Power/by Stuart A. Kallen.
Description: San Diego, CA: ReferencePoint Press, Inc., 2018. | Series: Real-World STEM | Includes bibliographical references and index.
Identifiers: LCCN 2017019497 (print) | LCCN 2017021940 (ebook) | ISBN 9781682822401 (eBook) | ISBN 9781682822395 (hardback)
Subjects: LCSH: Solar energy—Popular works.
Classification: LCC TJ810.3 (ebook) | LCC TJ810.3 .K35 2018 (print) | DDC 621.31/244--dc23
LC record available at https://lccn.loc.gov/2017019497

CONTENTS

Great Engineering Achievements

 Electrification
Vast networks of electricity provide power for the developed world.

 Automobile
Revolutionary manufacturing practices made cars more reliable and affordable, and the automobile became the world's major mode of transportation.

Airplane
Flying made the world accessible, spurring globalization on a grand scale.

Water Supply and Distribution
Engineered systems prevent the spread of disease, increasing life expectancy.

  Electronics
First with vacuum tubes and later with transistors, electronic circuits underlie nearly all modern technologies.

  Radio and Television
These two devices dramatically changed the way the world receives information and entertainment.

 Agricultural Mechanization
Numerous agricultural innovations led to a vastly larger, safer, and less costly food supply.

Computers
Computers are now at the heart of countless operations and systems that impact people's lives.

 Telephone
The telephone changed the way the world communicates personally and in business.

 Air Conditioning and Refrigeration
Beyond providing convenience, these innovations extend the shelf life of food and medicines, protect electronics, and play an important role in health care delivery.

Highways

Forty-four thousand miles of US highways enable personal travel and the wide distribution of goods.

Spacecraft

Going to outer space vastly expanded humanity's horizons and resulted in the development of more than sixty thousand new products on Earth.

Internet

The Internet provides a global information and communications system of unparalleled access.

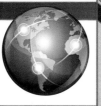

Imaging

Numerous imaging tools and technologies have revolutionized medical diagnostics.

Household Appliances

These devices have eliminated many strenuous and laborious tasks.

Health Technologies

From artificial implants to the mass production of antibiotics, these technologies have led to vast health improvements.

Laser and Fiber Optics

Their applications are wide and varied, including almost simultaneous worldwide communications, noninvasive surgery, and point-of-sale scanners.

Petroleum and Petrochemical Technologies

These technologies provided the fuel that energized the twentieth century.

Nuclear Technologies

From splitting the atom came a new source of electric power.

High-Performance Materials

They are lighter, stronger, and more adaptable than ever before.

Source: Wm. A. Wulf, "Great Achievements and Grand Challenges," National Academy of Engineering, *The Bridge*, Fall/Winter 2000. www.nae.edu.

Power from the Sun

"We need to invest dramatically in green energy, making solar panels so cheap that everybody wants them. Nobody wanted to buy a computer in 1950, but once they got cheap, everyone bought them."

—Bjørn Lomborg, scientist

Quoted in Sophie Elmhirst, "The NS Interview: Bjørn Lomborg," *New Statesman,* September 24, 2010. www.newstatesman.com.

Every living thing on Earth depends upon the sun for survival. Every day the heat and light of the sun sends thirty-five thousand times more energy to Earth than all human power consumption combined. If it was possible to utilize all the solar energy hitting Earth in a single twenty-four-hour period, there would be enough power to fuel industrial civilization for twenty-seven years.

Although scientists, mathematicians, and engineers cannot harvest 100 percent of the sun's energy, great strides have been made in turning solar rays into electricity since the first solar panel was produced in 1954. During the 1990s commercially available solar panels were not very efficient; they could convert around 15 percent of the sun's energy to electricity. Solar panels, referred to as photovoltaic (PV) cells, produced in 2017 were 24 percent efficient. At the same time that efficiency has increased, the price of solar panels has dropped dramatically; the cost of an average home solar system has gone from around $53,000 in 2002 to $20,000 in 2017. And today numerous government tax breaks worth thousands of dollars make solar systems even cheaper. These factors have spurred major growth in the multibillion-dollar solar energy industry.

WORDS IN CONTEXT

photovoltaic

relating to the production of electric current in a substance exposed to light

While homeowners install rooftop solar panels, large energy companies are building and operating massive solar farms. Each one of these large-scale photovoltaic power stations produces enough electricity to supply hundreds of thousands of customers. The largest photovoltaic power stations are located in China, India, and the United States, but solar farms are operating in more than a dozen nations, including Chile, France, Germany, Australia, and Japan.

With more photovoltaic power stations and rooftop solar installations, the amount of electricity provided by the sun continues to grow. According to the research company GlobalData, around 1 percent of the world's total energy needs came from solar panels in 2017. Although that percentage might not sound

An aerial view of a solar farm in the southwestern United States offers a unique perspective. Solar farms operate in many nations around the world including China, India, the United States, Germany, Chile, and Japan.

like much, the number is expected to grow in the near future. According to the *Solar PV Atlas* report by the environmental group World Wildlife Fund, solar could provide 30 percent of global electricity by 2050.

Solving Problems ■

Considerable progress has been made in lowering costs and improving efficiency in solar panels. But solar energy will not produce 30 percent of the world's electricity, or even 10 percent, until further improvements are made. Researchers and engineers need to make solar panels even less expensive and more efficient while also finding better ways to store the excess power produced during the day.

The term *photovoltaic* relates to the production of electric current in a substance exposed to light (*photo* means "light" and *voltaic* means "electricity"). Photovoltaic cells create electricity when sunlight hits semiconductors located inside the panel. Semiconductors—devices that conduct electricity—are made from silicon, an element that can be found in sand. All modern digital devices, including computers, televisions, and smartphones, rely on microchips made from semiconductors. These devices use tiny semiconductors. For example, the microprocessor that governs all functions of an Apple iPhone 6 is smaller than a dime. However, a single household rooftop solar cell is 39 inches by 65 inches (1 m by 1.6 m)—and the entire surface is covered with semiconductors. Semiconductors of this size are very expensive to produce, as is the equipment needed to convert their output into household electricity.

> **WORDS IN CONTEXT**
>
> **semiconductor**
>
> a substance, usually a solid chemical element or compound, that can conduct electricity under some conditions but not others

Of course, the major drawback to solar cells is they need sunshine to work. On cloudy days a typical solar panel only produces 10 to 25 percent of its capacity, and the cells do not produce power at night. Solar energy can be stored in batteries, but these expensive power storage units drive up the cost of the systems and make the price of solar energy even higher.

Solar Singularity ■

Most consumers who install solar panels are willing to put up with the expense and limitations of solar power in order to reduce the amount of carbon dioxide (CO_2) they produce—known as their carbon footprint. When coal, petroleum, and natural gas are burned, they create carbon dioxide, which is a significant contributor to climate change. In 2015 coal and natural gas power plants contributed to 37 percent of all CO_2 emissions in the United States, according to the Energy Information Administration. Worldwide fossil fuel power generation was responsible for 25 percent of all CO_2 emissions.

The urgent need to address climate change is motivating scientists and researchers to improve solar cells, build better solar power utilities, and create more reliable solar energy storage systems. Proponents say these combined efforts will one day create what scientists call solar singularity. This phrase describes an era when energy from the sun is so cheap and efficient that solar is the only power source anyone would consider using in homes, businesses, cars, and large-scale power facilities. Some researchers predict solar singularity will occur by 2040, but others expect it to happen sooner. Whenever it occurs, harnessing solar power in an efficient and affordable manner is one of the biggest scientific challenges of the twenty-first century.

CHAPTER 1

CURRENT STATUS:
Sunlight to Electricity

"The sun shows up every day and produces ridiculous amounts of power."

—Elon Musk, engineer and inventor

Quoted in Gina Coplon-Newfield, "5 Things You May Have Missed About Elon Musk's Tesla Battery Announcement," EcoWatch, May 9, 2015. http://ecowatch.com.

In the early 1900s, scientists understood that the chemical selenium could produce an electric current when exposed to sunlight, but no one knew why. It took the genius of theoretical physicist Albert Einstein to explain the phenomenon. Einstein was twenty-six years old when he wrote a paper describing the photoelectric effect in 1905. Einstein wrote that sunlight is made up of particles called photons that generate electrical energy. For example, when the eye absorbs a photon, the electrical energy is transmitted to the brain in the form of an image. Likewise, when a photon strikes certain types of metal, the energy produced by the collision releases electrons that can be converted into heat or electricity.

Einstein won the Nobel Prize in Physics in 1921 for discovering what is called the law of the photoelectric effect. But it was not until the 1950s that Bell Laboratories used the law to create the first photovoltaic cell. Bell was searching for a way to provide power to telephones in remote locations. Researchers discovered that they could combine the elements silicon, arsenic, and boron to create what is called a positive-negative (p-n) junction. An electrical field is created when an excess positive charge builds up on one side of the junction and an excessive

WORDS IN CONTEXT

photoelectric

the emission of electrons caused by light hitting a surface

negative charge builds up on the other side. When photons from sunlight hit the p-n junction, the extra electrons in the silicon are ejected, which causes a current to start flowing. Bell used this discovery to create the first solar cells, which were linked together in rectangular panels that resemble modern solar collectors. Bell called the device a solar battery.

Bell Laboratories put on a public demonstration of the solar battery on April 25, 1954, powering a small toy Ferris wheel and a radio transmitter. A *New York Times* reporter attended the event and wrote that the invention of the Bell solar battery "may mark the beginning of a new era, leading eventually to the realization of one of mankind's most cherished dreams—the harnessing of the almost limitless energy of the sun for the uses of civilization."[1] The *Times* reporter was overly optimistic; the solar cells were expensive to produce—about $2,000 in today's money for a small battery. Due to the expense, Bell had a difficult time marketing the battery for industrial purposes.

Although solar batteries were not commercially viable on Earth, the National Aeronautics and Space Administration (NASA) was quick to understand the value of solar power. In 1958 the NASA satellite *Vanguard 1* was the first to be equipped with solar

The world's first solar-powered satellite, Vanguard 1, *undergoes maintenance in Florida in 1958. Early work done by NASA on solar power led to many advances that have benefitted both the US space program and consumers.*

cells; a small array, or group of photovoltaic cells, was used to power its radios. In the years that followed, the space agency spent millions of dollars to improve solar technology so that it could be reliably used to power spacecraft sent to the moon and planets beyond.

NASA's research into solar power led to the development of small solar cells that were incorporated into consumer goods. The first solar wristwatch was produced in 1970 while sun-powered calculators began to appear in stores in 1978. However, rooftop solar panels remained prohibitively expensive. It was not until the early twenty-first century that technological advances in solar cell production led to increased efficiency and lower cost.

The Photovoltaic Cell ■

Modern photovoltaic cells are made from silicon semiconductors. A semiconductor is a crystal that is constructed to regulate power in electronic circuits. The transistors and microprocessors used in modern electronics are semiconductors. A standard photovoltaic cell consists of two extremely thin wafers of highly purified silicon sandwiched together. These wafers are around 0.01 inches (0.03 cm) thick and form a p-n junction. When photons hit the cell, the silicon absorbs the light and electrons are knocked loose, which in turn generates an electrical current. When the intensity of the light is greater, more photons are absorbed and more current is generated. Electrical conductors connected to the solar cell capture the electrons in the form of a direct current (DC), or current flowing in one direction.

A single photovoltaic cell is a basic unit that only produces a small amount of power. For a cell to be useful, it must be connected with other cells in what is called a module—a solar panel consisting of thirty-six interconnected cells. Modules are designed to protect thin and fragile solar cells, which are sandwiched between a front sheet, usually made of glass, and a backing sheet made from glass or tough plastic. This package prevents the cells from breaking and also protects them from rain, snow, blowing debris, and other weather conditions. The module is often encased in

Alternating Current and Direct Current

There are two types of electrical current: alternating current (AC) and direct current (DC). Alternating current is the form of electricity that powers lamps, televisions, computers, appliances, and other devices through wall sockets. AC is so named because it periodically cycles or reverses direction; in the United States, AC current cycles sixty times per second. This unit of frequency is referred to as sixty hertz. Outside the United States, most countries use fifty hertz of AC power. One advantage of AC is that the voltage—or intensity of the electric charge—can easily be increased and decreased. This allows AC power to be transmitted through high-voltage power lines. Before the current is directed into a household, it passes through a transformer to decrease the voltage to a safer level.

DC is not cycled—it only flows in one direction. Batteries and photovoltaic cells use DC, which produces constant voltage. DC is commonly used in what are called extra-low-voltage devices that have a very low risk of producing electrical shock.

an aluminum frame, which allows the unit to be anchored to the ground or attached to a roof. Any number of solar modules can be wired together into a larger system called an array. A typical home solar array consists of thirty modules.

Although solar cells produce DC power, most electrical devices, including lamps, microwaves, televisions, computers, and appliances, run on alternating current (AC), or current that periodically reverses direction. Solar power systems use a device called an inverter to convert DC solar power to AC power. Inverters take low-voltage DC signals from the solar panels and convert them into what is called 120 VAC (voltage in alternating current), which is compatible with the US electrical grid. (In Europe the standard is 230 VAC.) Inverters are expensive—those used in a typical home solar system cost around $2,600. Larger systems are even more expensive because they require several inverters.

Rooftop Solar ■

Most electricity provided by the sun is created by rooftop solar panels or large-scale solar power facilities. Rooftop solar can be found on individual homes and commercial buildings. These systems are measured by how many kilowatts of power they generate. One kilowatt is one thousand watts of electricity—enough to power ten one-hundred-watt lightbulbs. If those lightbulbs were powered for one hour, they would consume one thousand kilowatt-hours of electricity. A typical home uses thirty kilowatt-hours of electricity a day.

The average rooftop solar system is rated at five kilowatt-hours. If the sun shines six hours a day, a five-kilowatt-hour system would generate enough power to meet the needs of a typical home. However, this is not true in all cases, as journalist Jennifer Robison explains: "If your roof faces north, forget about it. Your panels won't

Rooftop solar panels provide electricity to houses located in sunny climates. Six hours of sunshine generates enough power to meet the needs of a typical house with a standard rooftop solar system.

see sunlight. Likewise, if your roof is broken up into multiple peaks and triangles—a common design for modern . . . homes—you might not have the rectangular roof expanse that solar panels need."[2]

Homeowners can use ground-based systems if their roofs are not ideal for solar panel placement. However, the amount of sunlight that a solar cell receives also depends on the season and location of the home. In the northern regions in the winter, the sun might shine a few hours a day or not at all. And solar energy needs to be stored for use at night. In such cases consumers can purchase rechargeable lithium-ion (or Li-ion) batteries that store electricity generated by solar panels. The Powerwall 2.0 storage battery, sold by the electric car company Tesla, can store 14 kilowatt-hours of electricity. The Powerwall 2.0 weighs 269 pounds (122 kg), is 5.5 inches (15 cm) thick, and is about 44 inches long and 29 inches wide (111 by 74 cm). The battery can be mounted on a wall in a garage or basement. In 2017 a Powerwall 2.0 with supporting hardware cost $6,250. An average household would need two Powerwall 2.0 storage batteries to provide all electricity needs when its solar panels are not producing power.

Lithium-Ion Batteries ■

In 2017 there were numerous brands of solar storage batteries available to consumers besides the Powerwall. Most large electronics companies, including Panasonic, Sony, and Samsung, sold lithium-ion batteries for consumers who wish to store excess solar power. These batteries work like the small lithium-ion batteries found in smartphones and laptop computers. All batteries store and release energy by moving electrons between two posts called electrodes. One electrode is called the anode; the other is called the cathode. The third battery ingredient, located between the electrodes, is called the electrolyte. When lithium-ion batteries are being charged, lithium ions from the cathode are driven through the electrolyte to the anode.

When a lithium-ion battery is being used, lithium ions in the electrolyte return to the cathode. As the ions move, electrons are released and the battery provides power to whatever electronic device may be attached. The concept can be compared to a waterwheel turned by the falling water of a stream. But instead of flowing water, lithium-ion batteries work with steadily moving electrons.

Lithium-ion batteries are widely used because they are energy dense, meaning they can store a lot of power in a lightweight, compact form. But the batteries also have disadvantages. Lithium is a highly volatile substance. If the battery is damaged or exposed to high heat, it can create a short circuit that causes the battery to overheat and burst into flames. Another problem with these batteries is that the cathode wears out over time. The process might be compared to an old rag that has been soaked and wrung out several hundred times; the cathode becomes threadbare on a molecular level as it is continually drained and recharged. Lithium-ion batteries become less powerful after one hundred charges and can fail completely after three to five hundred charges.

Large Modules with Thin Film ■

Consumers with storage batteries and rooftop solar panels are the most visible part of the solar revolution. But more than half of all solar capacity built in the United States between 2010 and 2015 was attributed to large-scale solar power systems connected to the electrical grid. More than twenty photovoltaic power stations were operational in the United States in 2017 and over thirty were in various stages of development.

Arizona's Agua Caliente solar facility was the world's largest photovoltaic power plant when it was completed in 2014. The Agua Caliente plant uses 4.9 million solar modules that spread across 2,400 acres (971 ha) of desert in Yuma County. The modules are made with thin-film solar cells. Thin film is a second-generation system made from a film of photovoltaic material that can be placed on glass, plastic, or metal. The semiconductors are made from a crystalline compound called cadmium telluride.

Thin-film solar cells are appropriately named; the material is only a few nanometers thick. There are over 25 million nanometers in 1 inch (2.5 cm), and a human hair is about 90,000 nanometers wide. The extreme thinness of thin-film cells means they are flexible and lightweight. Large solar power stations use

> **WORDS IN CONTEXT**
>
> **nanometer**
>
> a unit of length in the metric system, equal to one-billionth of a meter

Turbines and Generators

Thermodynamics is the study of the relationship between energy conversion and mechanical actions. An electrical turbine is based on thermodynamic principles. In a solar thermal energy facility, the heat of the sun is used to generate steam. The energy of the high-pressure steam is turned into mechanical energy when it causes a turbine to rotate. The mechanical energy of the turbine is converted into electrical energy by a generator that works in tandem with the turbine.

The generator is based on the principle of electromagnetic induction, discovered by British scientist Michael Faraday in 1831. Faraday learned that if he rotated a magnet within a loop of copper wire, electric current flowed through the wire. He also found the reverse was true. Rotating wire within a circle of magnets produced the same effect. On a turbine, the rotating mechanical energy turns a shaft on a generator. The shaft spins wire inside a magnetic field, which creates electric energy. The resulting electricity is fed into the power grid.

thin-film cells sandwiched between two pieces of glass. Thin-film solar cells are cheaper to produce and cost around half as much as first-generation silicon-based cells. However, cadmium telluride is less efficient than silicon and the material degrades faster, which gives the cells a shorter life span. Thin-film solar cells last about twenty years compared to thirty years for traditional solar cells.

Unlike the solar modules that are fixed in place on the roofs of homes, the modules at the Agua Caliente plant are motorized; they follow the sun as it tracks across the sky to absorb the strongest solar rays. The plant cost nearly $1 billion and generates 290 megawatts of power (one megawatt equals one thousand kilowatts) every hour when running at full capacity. This amount of electricity is enough to power 230,000 average homes.

Solar Thermal Energy ■

Although the Agua Caliente facility is huge, it relies on the conventional method to generate power: the plant's solar arrays convert photons into electrons. Other solar energy generating facilities use a different system that utilizes heat, or thermal, energy. These power generators are known as concentrated solar plants, and they use the concentrated heat of the sun to generate power.

Solar thermal energy systems use specialized moving mirrors, called heliostats, which reflect the heat of the sun as it tracks across the sky. The heliostats are set in a large circle around a tall structure called a power tower receiver. A boiler filled with water or a salt solution is located on top of the power tower. The heliostats focus concentrated solar heat on the boiler. The liquid inside is heated, creating high-temperature steam. The steam is piped to a turbine that spins a generator to produce electricity.

Research on solar thermal energy began in 1978 with the construction of the National Solar Thermal Test Facility in Albuquerque, New Mexico. The facility is run by Sandia National Laboratories, a research and development lab that is part of the US Department of Energy. By the mid-1980s the facility had finished construction of the central receiver power plant, consisting of 222 heliostats and a computer control system. In the decades that followed, scientists and engineers continued to improve on heliostat and power tower designs.

Research at the test facility resulted in usable commercial applications for solar thermal energy in 2007. At that time the Internet giant Google joined with two energy companies—BrightSource Energy and NRG Energy—to build a concentrated solar plant called the Ivanpah Solar Electric Generating System. Construction on the Ivanpah plant began in 2010 on a 4,000 acre (1,619 ha) site in California's Mojave Desert. The facility, located near the small town of Ivanpah, began generating power commercially in 2014.

The Ivanpah plant is capable of producing 392 megawatts of power. In 2017 it was the world's largest solar thermal power station. The facility uses 173,500 heliostats—each one deploying two mirrors the size of double garage doors. These devices focus the sun's energy on three centralized solar power towers that are filled with water. When running at peak efficiency, the Ivanpah complex generates enough electricity to power more than 140,000 homes. Proponents of the plant point out that the facility is having a positive impact on the environment; compared

The Ivanpah Solar Electric Generating System (pictured) is located in California's Mojave Desert. When running at peak efficiency, the world's largest solar thermal power station generates enough electricity to power more than 140,000 homes.

to a natural gas power plant, the Ivanpah facility reduces carbon dioxide emissions by more than 400,000 tons (362,874 t) per year, the equivalent of removing seventy thousand cars from the road annually.

Flying High ■

Although solar power is traditionally used to keep the power humming in homes and businesses, engineers at Ford Motor Company envision a day when the sun will be used to power all automobiles. In 2014 Ford developed the C-MAX Solar Energi Concept car powered by energy it collects using a special concentrator that works like a magnifying glass. The concentrator focuses the sun's energy from solar panels on the car's roof, which then charges onboard batteries.

Whatever the future may hold, there is little doubt that the sun can provide adequate power to keep homes and businesses working efficiently. In fact, the astronauts in the International Space Station have proved it. The station is attached to eight 114-foot (35 m) solar array wings. Each one contains thirty-three thousand solar cells that convert 14 percent of the sun's energy into electricity. This solar array produces enough power to provide all the electricity needed by the station's astronauts. And NASA has an entire division—the Photovoltaic & Space Environments Branch—dedicated to the task of making solar cells lighter, cheaper, and more efficient.

Trillions of photons hit the earth every second of the day, enough to power civilization for years. And it would not take much land to capture and convert that light energy into a useful form. As engineer and inventor Elon Musk told a group of engineers in Norway in 2014, "You could power the entire United States with about 150 to 200 square kilometers [58 to 77 sq. mi] of solar panels, the entire United States. Take a corner of Utah [and install solar panels]. . . . There's not much going on there, I've been there."[3] Such an installation would allow people to run their appliances, charge electric cars, and recharge storage batteries without burning fossil fuels. If the solar industry continues to grow as it has, Musk's dream might someday become reality.

CHAPTER 2

PROBLEMS:
Efficiency and Cost

"Even decades after they were first developed, the slabs of silicon [in solar cells] remain bulky, expensive, and inefficient. Fundamental limitations prevent these conventional photovoltaics from absorbing more than a fraction of the energy in sunlight."

—James Temple, editor of the *MIT Technology Review*

James Temple, "Hot Solar Cells," *MIT Technology Review*, March/April 2017. www.technologyreview.com.

Germany is a coal-rich country. During the early twenty-first century, about half of the nation's electricity was produced by coal. This cheap resource kept electric bills low for consumers and businesses that made steel and cars. The German government, however, wanted to drastically reduce the nation's carbon footprint. In 2002 laws were passed to require utility companies to purchase electricity from renewable wind and solar sources, whatever the cost. Because of the increased costs associated with producing power with solar cells, Germany's electric bills skyrocketed. In 2009 solar power plants charged eight times more for electricity than coal power plants.

Despite the cost, Germany became the world's largest solar market; in 2017 around 6.5 percent of all electricity in the nation was produced by photovoltaic cells. But this move to solar power came at a cost. According to the environmental news service Clean Energy Wire, Germany's household power prices reached record highs in 2017; German consumers were paying three times more for electricity than American consumers. Around eight hundred thousand Germans—1 percent of the population—had their power cut off because they could not afford to pay their electric bills.

The high price of renewable power has also hit Germany's industrial sector. Steel and automobile production make up 25 percent of the German economy. But some of these energy-intensive companies have been looking to move production to the United States, where electricity is cheaper.

Germany is providing a useful lesson to nations hoping to increase their reliance on solar power. Wherever it is used, solar is an expensive power source for several reasons. Although prices on solar cells have dramatically declined in recent years, there are costs associated with producing electricity from the sun that have nothing to do with the cost of the equipment.

Part-Time Electricity ■

The price of solar electricity is driven up by the fact that solar cells are outdoors and are affected by the seasons, atmospheric conditions, and other conditions that cannot be controlled. During late fall, winter, and early spring, the earth receives less solar radiation, especially in northern and southern regions. Clouds, snow, and rain reduce the ability of solar cells to produce electricity. Likewise, wind blows dirt and dust onto solar panels, reducing the amount of power they produce. A tiny dust deposit equal to 0.1 ounces (2.8 g) spread out across a square yard (0.8 sq. m) of a solar panel can reduce efficiency by as much as 40 percent.

These problems mean solar power is not reliable. Wherever it is used, a backup source of power is necessary. As Benjamin Sporton, chief executive officer of the World Coal Association, states, "Solar can only generate part-time, intermittent electricity. While some renewable technologies have achieved significant cost reductions in recent years, it's important to look at total system costs."[4] The overall costs are preventing solar power from gaining a larger share of the market. Solar accounts for only 1 percent all electricity generation worldwide. In the United States, residential, business, and utility solar power production has multiplied in recent years—rising from 334 megawatts in 1997 to 17,762 megawatts in 2016. However, this increase still accounts for only 0.6 percent of electricity generated

WORDS IN CONTEXT

intermittent

occurring at irregular intervals

in the United States. Even though the solar industry is growing rapidly, sun-powered systems in 2017 produced less electricity than renewable power systems like hydroelectric, wind, and geothermal.

Inefficiency and Reflection ■

If solar panels were more efficient, it might solve some of the problems associated with atmospheric conditions and weather. However, there are several factors that contribute to the inefficiency of solar cells. One problem is related to the reflection caused by the materials used to make the devices. The silicon used to make semiconductors can reflect as much sunlight as the sun hitting the surface of a lake. A bare silicon solar cell will reflect 30 percent

The Environmental Cost of Solar Panels

Solar cells are symbols of green energy that generate electricity with very little harm to the environment. However, there are environmental costs associated with solar cell production that are largely hidden from the public. Cell fabrication is an energy- and water-intensive process that requires the use of highly toxic chemicals. The basic element of a solar cell is silicon, which is hardened at high temperatures in giant furnaces that consume massive amounts of electricity. More than 60 percent of solar panels are made in China, where two-thirds of the electricity is produced by burning coal. A study by the Argonne National Laboratory in Illinois found that Chinese solar panels have twice the carbon footprint of those made in the United States. Although the panels help reduce carbon emissions over the long run, the high carbon intensity means it takes twice as long to compensate for greenhouse gas emissions created in production.

Solar cell production also generates chemical pollution. Highly corrosive compounds such as silicon tetrachloride and hydrofluoric acid are created during the manufacturing process. Cancer-causing heavy metals such as copper, cadmium telluride, and cadmium sulfide are also used. Workers are sometimes exposed to these dangerous chemicals; the toxins also find their way into the environment through mishandling or intentional dumping. Responsible manufacturers handle these toxic compounds safely, but they pay added costs to protect their employees and the environment. Thus, by ignoring safety procedures, less reputable companies are often able to produce cheaper solar cells.

of the energy that it receives. However, most cells are treated with an antireflective coating, which reduces reflection to 10 percent.

Another source of reflection is traced to the shiny surface metals that are part of the solar panel structure. This metal reduces efficiency by around 4 percent. There is also a loss of efficiency created by metal wires that cover around 7 percent of the top surface of a solar cell. These wires reduce efficiency by around 5 percent, but they perform the necessary function of carrying electricity to and from the solar cell. As materials scientist Yi Cui explains, "The more metal you have on the surface, the more light you block. That light is then lost and cannot be converted to electricity."[5]

When all reflection problems are added up, total solar cell efficiency is reduced by nearly one-fifth. Manufacturers have used various techniques to create more efficient solar panels, but they are extremely expensive; a 35 percent efficient panel manufactured by Spectrolab in 2014 cost $100,000 per square yard.

Competing with Cheaper Forms of Energy ■

Efficiency is not a problem for large-scale solar facilities where mirrors, power towers, and other technology creates concentrated heat to power electrical generators. However, operators of these facilities faced financial problems in 2017 because cheaper forms of energy dominated the energy market. The $2.2 billion Ivanpah Solar Electric Generating System in California is a good example. Electricity prices are measured in cents per kilowatt-hour. When the Ivanpah facility was first proposed in 2007, natural gas power plants produced electricity for around fifteen cents per kilowatt-hour. The Ivanpah plant could produce electricity for the same amount. However, by 2016 there was a glut of natural gas. Power plants that operated with natural gas were selling electricity for four cents per kilowatt-hour. Ivanpah's operators could not lower their prices because they needed to pay back billions of dollars in construction loans used to build the facility. This would be impossible at four cents per kilowatt-hour, or even ten cents.

Ivanpah was also competing with consumers who were installing cheap rooftop solar panels; the cost of electricity from home solar systems hit a record low of six cents per kilowatt-hour in 2016. As energy analyst Adam Schultz says, "You're not going to see the same [lower prices] with a concentrated solar power plant because it's mostly just a big steel and glass project. It can only get so much cheaper."[6] Ivanpah had other problems as well. In May 2016 one of the power towers burst into flames because the mirrors did not track the sun properly, focusing sunlight on the wrong parts of the tower. No one was injured, but the fire knocked out one-third of the plant's generating capabilities for several months, causing further financial difficulties for the struggling solar facility.

The negative forces working against Ivanpah were seen at other large-scale solar facilities. BrightSource Energy, which co-owns the Ivanpah facility, canceled a proposed five-hundred-megawatt concentrated solar project planned for Inyo County, California. And the Spanish company Abengoa, which developed several large concentrated solar projects, filed for bankruptcy in 2016. As Richard Martin, an editor of the *MIT Technology Review* explains, "The [solar thermal] process has certain advantages over solar photovoltaic technology, including higher efficiencies in terms of the amount of solar energy converted to electricity, but in today's low-cost environment it's simply too expensive."[7]

The Grid Problem ■

If Ivanpah could sell its power to customers in cloudy northern states, it might be more profitable. However, when electricity is sent through transmission lines, a substantial amount of the power is lost. The further the electricity is transmitted, the greater the loss. This effect is called leakage, and it means that power generated at concentrated solar facilities in the sunny Mojave Desert cannot be efficiently transmitted to New York or Chicago. The leakage problem contributed to the cancellation of a massive solar power plant in the Sahara Desert in northern Africa. The facility was slated to supply 15 percent of Europe's energy by 2050. But the plan collapsed in 2016 because it made no sense to transmit the solar power for thousands of miles to customers in Europe.

Transmission lines make up one part of the electrical grid, which was created over the course of many decades to deliver electricity from large, centralized power plants to homes and businesses. The grid consists of interconnected networks that carry power through high-voltage transmission lines, distribution lines, substations, switches, and transformers.

The electrical grid is sometimes referred to as the world's greatest machine, but it was never built to be compatible with rooftop solar systems. In the United States around 1 million peo-

> **WORDS IN CONTEXT**
>
> **substation**
>
> a facility that contains transformers and other equipment that reduces high voltage electrical power to low voltage for consumer use

ple had solar power systems in 2016. Millions of similar systems could be found throughout the industrialized world. Each one of these systems is attached to an inverter to convert the DC solar electricity into AC power for the home's electrical system.

Inverters are designed to use the solar power first; if solar panels are not producing enough electricity for the demand, the inverter switches to the grid. Conversely, if the home's solar system is creating more electric energy than the consumer needs, the inverter sends that power into the grid. In some places utilities pay consumers for this electricity, an activity known as net metering. The grids in almost every developed

Transmission lines make up one part of the electrical grid, which is the system that brings power to homes and businesses. At present, solar power cannot be fully integrated into the electrical grid.

nation, however, were built during the last century and were not designed to handle net metering from thousands of private solar systems.

Net metering stresses the electric grid because solar power is inconsistent. For a power grid to function properly, the demand for energy must match the supply exactly. The output of conventional power plants can be strictly regulated so that supply matches demand. However, when thousands of rooftop solar panels generate excess power during the day, this oversupply can overload the grid and even cause it to fail. And solar power production fluctuates—too much is produced at midday, but the supply drops drastically at sunset. According to solar analyst Yan Qin, the main

Acres of Land for Megawatts of Power

Large-scale solar plants present environmental challenges because they occupy large areas of land. According to the Union of Concerned Scientists, a large solar facility requires 3.5 to 10 acres (1.5 to 4 ha) for every megawatt of power produced. A solar thermal system can take up between 4 and 16 acres (1.6 to 6.4 ha) per megawatt. This means a one-thousand-megawatt solar thermal system can cover 4,000 to 16,000 acres (1,618 to 6,474 ha). (By way of comparison, a football field is 1.3 acres, or 0.5 hectares.) A natural gas electric plant with the same capacity would take up 40 to 80 acres (16 to 32 ha). According to nuclear engineer Mehran Moalem, if it were possible to power the entire world with solar energy, it would require 43,000 square miles (111,369 sq. km) of solar panels, an area the size of Virginia. And an equal area of land would be needed for service roads and support facilities.

Proponents of large-scale solar facilities suggest building them on land that is already disturbed. Solar facilities could be constructed on abandoned mining land, corridors along roadways, or brownfields contaminated by industrial pollution. However, critics point out that many large solar plants are often built in environmentally sensitive places. For example, the Ivanpah Solar Electric Generating System in California was built on 5 square miles (13 sq. km) of the Mojave Desert that was considered critical habitat for endangered desert tortoises.

problem for solar expansion in the future is "grid infrastructure, which was built to carry fairly consistent levels of generation and will struggle to cope with the variability of solar . . . energy."[8]

This grid problem could be solved by building a new generation of power plants with what is called ramping capabilities. These plants can rapidly adjust power output to match the rising and falling waves of solar power generation. Construction of a smart electrical grid would also address the ramping issues. A smart grid would employ a computerized network with millions of sensors connected to devices on the network. The sensors would gather data from thousands of solar panels, power meters, voltage detectors, traditional power plants, wind turbines, and other energy sources. The sensors would constantly communicate with a centralized utility to adjust and control each of the millions of devices connected to the smart grid. According to German energy consultant Daniel Genz, "If you want to use fluctuating renewable power, you have to upgrade the grids."[9] However, the construction of new ramping power plants and a smart grid would be incredibly expensive. Planners with the European Union (EU) are hoping to construct a so-called supergrid by 2050 that would connect large and small power generators throughout the continent. According to an EU report, the supergrid would cost between $112 billion and $488 billion.

Science and energy professor Seth Blumsack worries that there will not be enough money to pay for large-scale improvements to power grids because homeowners with rooftop solar systems do not pay the utilities for their power: "There is thus the potential to create a type of 'death spiral.' The more homeowners that install rooftop solar, the more expensive the grid maintenance costs become for everyone else, which in turn encourages more homeowners to install solar panels to avoid higher utility costs."[10]

The Promise and the Reality ■

Some utilities have proposed charging consumers with rooftop solar panels a monthly fee for grid maintenance, but this idea is strongly rejected by the solar industry. However, maintaining a healthy electric grid remains in the best interests of consumers—until better solar storage batteries are developed. But like other solar energy systems, the promise of rechargeable solar storage batteries has not met expectations. When Tesla's Elon Musk introduced the Powerwall in 2015 he said, "Our goal is to fundamentally change the way the world uses energy. It sounds crazy, but we want to change the entire energy infrastructure of the world to zero carbon."[11]

Musk painted a picture of a future in which every home is powered by lithium-ion batteries charged with renewable solar energy. However, simple math shows why this concept is not realistic. In sunny southern climates a clean, properly positioned solar array efficiently creates electricity an average of six hours a day, providing it is not cloudy, raining, or snowing. (During the several hours after sunrise and before sunset, solar panels are minimally efficient.) Most of the power produced in those six hours is consumed by lights and household appliances. If the homeowner wanted to use solar power twenty-four hours a day, it would require the addition of three more solar cells solely to recharge batteries during those six sunny hours. Two fourteen-kilowatt-hour Powerwall 2.0 batteries would cost $12,500. If it is cloudy for several consecutive days—or weeks—the batteries will be useless and the homeowner will have to rely on the grid for power. And the picture is worse for consumers who live in northern regions such as New York State, where on average there are only three full hours a day with enough sunlight to generate electricity. As science writer Sarah Zhang notes, "Solar panels produce energy when the sun is shining, and they're basically roof decorations when it's not."[12]

Simple math is also the reason why millions of people are not mounting solar panels on their roofs. Solar energy does not pencil out—that is, it does not make economic sense for homeowners who do not plan to keep their homes for at least twenty-five years. According to the US Department of Energy, the average monthly electric bill in the United States in 2016 was $114. At this rate a consumer would have to produce nine years of free solar electricity just to break even on the cost of two Powerwall batteries. It would take another twelve years to pay for a rooftop solar system costing $16,500. Add in the cost of a $2,600 inverter and it would take a homeowner twenty-one years before breaking even on the investment in a solar power system. Federal and state govern-

Coal-fired power plants like this one in England emit carbon dioxide into the atmosphere. Converting to solar power would significantly reduce carbon emissions, which scientists have linked to climate change.

ments provide tax credits to those who install solar systems that amount to around $5,000 but solar energy remains a long-term investment that does not pay off financially for many years.

Some people are motivated by the environmental benefits of solar power; an average solar power system prevents 5,760 pounds (2,613 kg) of carbon dioxide pollution from going into the atmosphere every year. Even when the CO_2 emissions associated with manufacturing solar cells are included, solar power is twenty times cleaner than coal. That is why environmentalists who can afford to invest in solar systems do so. However, that category is small according to former General Motors vice chairman Bob Lutz: "Surveys show that maybe 4 or 5% of Americans feel so deeply about climate change and the environment that they're willing to make a [financial] sacrifice."[13] And consumers are not the only ones who will need to sacrifice to make solar power practical. Billions of research dollars will need to be invested—and trillions of dollars will have to be spent for grid improvements—before the dream of cheap solar power for all becomes a reality.

CHAPTER 3

SOLUTIONS:
Improving Solar Cells

"We have an enormous resource in the sun. If we could utilize the sunlight one hundred per cent, an hour of the annual sunlight would meet all the energy needs on Earth."

—Bengt Svensson, physics professor

Quoted in Yngve Vogt, "Nano Tricks Boost Solar Cell Efficiency," *Controlled Environments,* March 27, 2017. www.cemag.us.

Solar energy is referred to as a mature technology. There is more than sixty years of research behind the power source. The manufacturing processes and materials used for solar cells have remained largely unchanged for the past several decades. But this is beginning to change. Scientists and engineers are combining creative engineering techniques with new types of materials to create the next generation of solar energy devices. These reimagined photovoltaic cells offer vast improvements over mature solar technology and capture far more energy from the sun.

Many of the developments are based on materials science, with research focused on new types of metals, chemicals, and semiconductors used in solar panels. Some of the science employs nanotechnology, which is the manipulation of matter on an atomic or molecular level. Advances in materials science are allowing researchers to harvest energy from a broader spectrum of light and from heat produced by solar radiation. These technological advances aim to make solar cells more efficient, smaller, and cheaper to produce.

Harvesting Blue Light ■
Every solar panel made since the 1950s, and nearly every one manufactured today, is made from silicon. In 2017 commercially

produced silicon cells harvested around 24 percent of sunlight—the theoretical limit is 32 percent. The limit is due to the fact that silicon can only capture visible light waves from the red portion of the spectrum of sunlight. Visible light is defined as wavelengths of electromagnetic radiation visible to the human eye. In addition to red light, the eye can perceive the other colors of the rainbow—orange, yellow, green, blue, and violet. Together these wavelengths make up only 7 percent of sunlight. Wavelengths of infrared and ultraviolet light, which are not visible to the human

Photovoltaic cells made from silicon are being assembled into solar panels. Silicon has been used for this purpose since the 1950s.

eye, make up the other 93 percent of solar radiation. Cutting-edge research into solar energy is focused on harvesting energy from the light waves that are not being utilized by today's solar cells.

In 2017 Norwegian researchers at the University of Oslo devised a way to double the efficiency of solar cells by harvesting energy from two wavelengths of visible light instead of one. The prototype solar cells are known as tandem cells. They combine

Lowering Costs with a Tofu Ingredient

Cadmium chloride, a chemical compound, has long been used to coat solar cells because it increases the efficiency of silicon by about 15 percent. But cadmium chloride is one of the most toxic substances used in the production of solar cells. The chemical has been linked to cancer, lung disease, and cardiovascular problems. Workers who use cadmium chloride must wear protective gear and take elaborate safety measures when working with the compound. The chemical residue needs to be handled as hazardous waste. These problems increase the cost of manufacturing solar cells. In addition, cadmium chloride is relatively expensive, costing around $135 a pound in 2016.

Physicist Jon Major of the University of Liverpool in England was searching for a compound that could be substituted for cadmium chloride when he discovered that magnesium chloride worked just as well. Magnesium chloride is extracted from seawater. Also known as nigari, the chemical is used to produce tofu, a food product made from soybeans. Magnesium chloride is also used in bath salts and deicing chemicals sprayed on roadways. It is nontoxic, abundant, and costs about three hundred times less than cadmium chloride. The chemical can even be applied to solar panels using inexpensive spray coaters purchased on the Internet. Major commented on the breakthrough: "Cadmium chloride is toxic, and expensive and we no longer need to use it. Replacing it with a naturally occurring substance could save the industry a vast amount of money and reduce the overall cost for generating power from solar."

Quoted in Phys.org, "Tofu Ingredient Could Revolutionise Solar Panel Manufacture," June 26, 2014. https://phys.org.

two layers of chemicals to capture different parts of the light spectrum. A silicon layer captures red light waves, and a copper oxide layer harvests light waves from the blue spectrum. Both layers of the solar cell are made of nanoparticles, which are exceptionally thin. The individual layers vary between one hundred and one thousand nanometers in thickness, less than 1 percent the width of a human hair.

Although the silicon layer cannot be made much more efficient, the copper oxide layer is capable of capturing 9 percent of the sun's blue rays. And researchers believe they can boost that number to 20 percent. Bengt Svensson, a physics professor and lead researcher on the project, describes the breakthrough: "The combination of silicon cells in the one layer and copper oxide cells in the other means that we'll be able to absorb far more light and thereby reduce the energy loss. With this combination, we can utilize 35 to 40 percent of the sunlight."[14]

The heightened efficiency of the tandem solar cells is due to an increase in what is called the band gap. Band gaps have to do with how electrons behave and what it takes to get them excited. Electrons are the subatomic particles that surround the nucleus of an atom and carry a negative charge. The nucleus of each atom has several bands around it. One of those bands is called the valence band, and it keeps electrons tightly in place. The next band out is called the conduction band, and it is where the electrons move around freely. In silicon and various other solid materials, electrons get excited when hit by light particles. This causes electrons to jump across the band gap from the valence band to the conduction band, where they are free to form an electric current. Silicon has a moderate band gap; it is just wide enough so that electrons can cross the band gap when hit by photons of visible light.

The band gap in silicon limits its efficiency; when an electron jumps the band gap, a tiny electron hole is left behind. In silicon, the electrons that do not jump the band gap when hit by light fall back into the electron holes and are not used to produce power.

> **WORDS IN CONTEXT**
>
> **band gap**
>
> the space between the valence and conduction bands that controls the movement of electrons around the nucleus of an atom

Substances made from copper oxide nanoparticles have an improved efficiency because the band gap is exactly the right size to capture a larger number of electrons before they fall back into electron holes.

Researchers believe that the copper oxide nanotechnology will soon be available for manufacturing purposes. As Svensson explains, "The technology is inexpensive, it can easily be scaled up to large volumes, and it's not more expensive to produce solar cells out of copper oxide than out of silicon."[15]

A Better, Cheaper Material ■

British researcher Henry Snaith believes he can increase the efficiency of silicon solar cells to 30 percent for only a few dollars per square yard. The basis for his research is the chemical compound calcium titanate, which was discovered in Russia in 1839 by a mineralogist named Lev Perovski. Calcium titanate, known as perovskite, has a unique quality; its band gap can be fine-tuned to harvest photons of blue and green light when the chemical is layered on top of silicon.

The efficiencies of solar cell devices using perovskite have skyrocketed since Japanese researchers first discovered the photovoltaic qualities of the material in 2009. At that time perovskite only converted around 4 percent of light energy into electricity. But researchers repeatedly improved the chemical recipe during the manufacturing process. By 2016 scientists were able to push the efficiency of perovskite past 22 percent. This gain in efficiency qualifies for the fastest advance in solar technology ever achieved.

When perovskite is layered in tandem with silicon, the prototypes have reached a 25.2 percent level of efficiency. And as science writer Robert F. Service explains, there are expectations that the efficiency level can go even higher: "Researchers have yet to build in all the finer tricks of the trade, such as optimizing the electricity-carrying layers in the cells and adding coatings that minimize surface reflections. Even with current perovskite materials, over the next couple years silicon-perovskite tandems could reach efficiencies of 30%."[16]

Perovskite is extremely cheap to make because the material can be created at low temperatures in a traditional lab setting.

This process differs from silicon, which requires an expensive multistep manufacturing process using high-temperature furnaces and special clean rooms that are free of dust, airborne pollutants, and microscopic particles that can contaminate semiconductors.

Snaith believes that improvements in perovskite cell production might advance so far that the chemical will completely replace silicon cells: "Perovskite is a better material. . . . It's easier to process, and it should be more efficient. We're close to a tipping point where conventional power [from fossil fuels] becomes not just un-environmental, but economically unfeasible."[17]

Heat into Power ■

While some researchers work to harvest more energy from the visible light spectrum, others are concentrating on converting the heat of the sun into electrical power. Thermal energy goes unused by common solar cells, but in 2017 researchers at the Massachusetts Institute of Technology were working to change that. The scientists devised a way to pair conventional solar cells with high-tech materials that can double the efficiency of the

silicon semiconductor by absorbing solar heat. The devices are called solar thermophotovoltaics (STPVs).

Unused heat from the sun is dissipated in traditional solar cells. In STPVs all of the sun's heat is absorbed by a substance made of carbon nanotubes, which take in the entire visible light spectrum. Carbon nanotubes are made from graphene, an extremely thin substance made from graphite. Under a microscope carbon nanotubes resemble sheets of flat carbon, one atom thick, rolled into incredibly tiny tubes (like drinking straws) with a diameter of one to one hundred nanometers—around one thousand times thinner than a human hair.

When the sun hits carbon nanotubes, all of the energy from the photons gets converted to heat; the carbon nanotubes operate at temperatures of 1,832°F (1,000°C). The heat is transferred to another nanomaterial called nanophotonic crystals, where it is

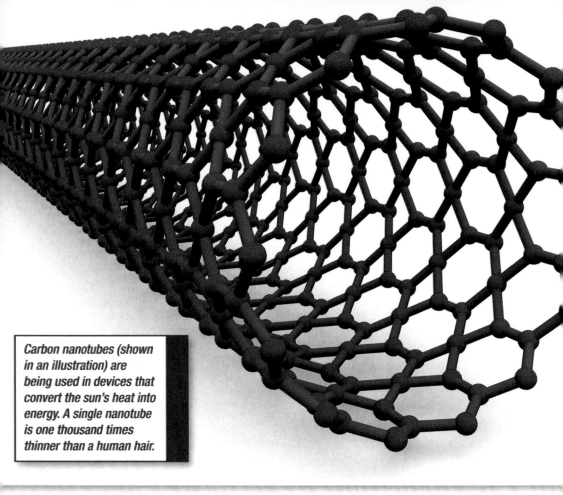

Carbon nanotubes (shown in an illustration) are being used in devices that convert the sun's heat into energy. A single nanotube is one thousand times thinner than a human hair.

reemitted as extremely precise wavelengths of light. The narrow bands of light waves precisely match the bandwidth that a nearby solar collector can most efficiently capture and convert into electricity. Unwanted wavelengths of light are reflected back to the carbon nanotubes where they continue to maintain the heat.

The main advantage of STPV systems is that they produce energy from heat as well as light. This means that STPVs can continue to produce full power when clouds pass in front of the sun. Researchers are also working on ways to store the heat in a thermal battery system, which would allow the STPVs to produce power at night. According to David Bierman, lead researcher on the project, "[This] could in principle provide a way to make use of solar power on an around-the-clock basis. . . . The biggest advantage is the promise of continuous on-demand power."[18]

STPVs are still in the experimental stage. Scientists have focused their research on finding ways to scale up the small, laboratory-sized experimental units. There are also plans to develop manufacturing techniques that would produce STPV systems in an economical manner.

The Blackness of Vantablack ■

Carbon nanotubes have many properties that make them useful for converting sunlight into electricity. At the National Physics Laboratory in the United Kingdom, researchers discovered in 2014 that aligning carbon nanotubes in a vertical manner produced the blackest artificial substance ever created. The researchers called it Vantablack, which stands for vertically aligned nanotube arrays. Vantablack is made from millions of carbon nanotubes, each one measuring twenty nanometers.

Black is the darkest color because it absorbs most light. (White reflects most light.) Vantablack could be considered superblack—it absorbs 99.96 percent of all radiation in the visible light spectrum along with ultraviolet and infrared light. No other substance is as black. Researchers discovered that adding a layer of Vantablack to the back of solar cells prevents sunlight from bouncing off the cell, improving efficiency by 8 percent. Vantablack solar cells could be particularly useful in northern climates, as Finnish researcher Hele Savin states: "This is an advantage particularly in the north, where the sun shines from a low angle for a large part of the year. We have demonstrated that in winter Helsinki, [Vantablack] cells generate considerably more electricity than traditional cells even though both cells have identical efficiency values."[19]

Although Vantablack could improve solar cell efficiency, it is expensive to manufacture; the substance is grown onto a surface using high heat over the course of several days. The material will exist as an experimental novelty until researchers can find cheaper production methods.

Printable Quantum Dots ■

Carbon nanotubes are extremely small, but quantum dots are even smaller. Quantum dots are crystals that function as semiconductors on an atomic level. They are described as artificial atoms, made up of only 100 to 100,000 atoms (a single grain of salt has 12 trillion atoms). The band gap of the dots can be finely tuned by changing their size. Quantum dots of the smallest size absorb blue light. As they get progressively larger, they absorb green, orange, and red light. The largest quantum dots absorb infrared light, which makes up nearly half of the solar energy reaching the earth.

Quantum dots are nontoxic and invisible to the naked eye. They are inexpensive because they can be manufactured in bulk, eliminating the chemical and energy-intensive manufacturing processes used to make silicon solar cells. The dots are synthesized using what is called wet chemistry; this involves heating a beaker and adding a chemical reactant. The crystals grow as long as the mixture is hot. Using precisely regulated temperatures, scientists can grow dots to different sizes.

Quantum dots are already being used in high-quality flat-screen televisions known as QLEDs, which are celebrated for their pure colors and extremely realistic images. In 2017 researchers at the Los Alamos Center for Advanced Solar Photophysics were using quantum dots to harvest solar energy. A thin film of quan-

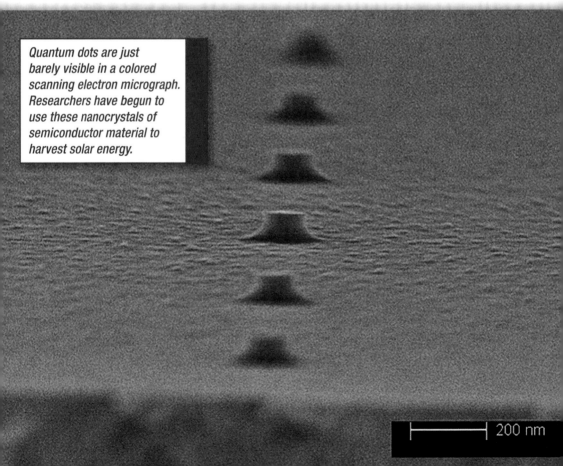

Quantum dots are just barely visible in a colored scanning electron micrograph. Researchers have begun to use these nanocrystals of semiconductor material to harvest solar energy.

200 nm

tum dots can be painted or sprayed onto roofing shingles, plastic panels, window glass, or other surfaces. The dots can even be printed on materials using a standard inkjet printer.

When quantum dots are sprayed on a window, they absorb a fraction of the light that passes through the glass. These nanoparticles then emit the solar energy as light particles invisible to the human eye. The light waves are guided to a solar cell at the edge of the window, where they are transformed into electricity. As Victor Klimov, a lead researcher at Los Alamos, explains, "Using this design, a nearly transparent window becomes an electrical generator, one that can power your room's air conditioner on a hot day or a heater on a cold one."[20]

The printed cells are only about 10.7 percent efficient. This amount might not sound that impressive, but the low cost of quantum dots and ease of manufacturing them would eliminate the need for expensive solar cells in many applications. As tech writer Tina Casey explains, "If the idea is to saturate the energy landscape with solar panels within a relatively short amount of time, then the highest-efficiency solar panels are not necessarily going to do the trick. . . . The idea behind the [quantum dot] research is to find a relatively abundant, low cost solar material that can be used in a high-volume manufacturing process."[21]

Trapping Light in Nanocones ■

Despite the advantages of spray-on quantum dots, questions about their durability remain. A conventional solar cell lasts up to thirty years, and some researchers believe the dot material is too fragile to last that long. As scientist Rana Biswas states, "Silicon solar cells today account for more than 90 percent of all installations worldwide. The industry is very skeptical that any other material could be as stable as silicon."[22] This doubt led Biswas to search for ways to create a new generation of ultrathin silicon solar cells that could compete in efficiency and strength with conventional thin-film silicon cells currently in use.

Thin-film solar cells are second-generation products that are made by attaching photovoltaic film to a base of glass, plastic, or other substance. Although thin-film solar cells are cheap to produce, they are only 12 to 14 percent efficient. The lower efficiency is due to the thinness of the film, which is only one micron

Printing Solar Cells

Traditional silicon solar cells are complicated and time-consuming to produce, which in turn drives up the cost of the electricity they produce. But the next generation of nonsilicon thin-film solar cells will be much cheaper to make. The cells will be printed on long rolls of aluminum foil using large presses like those used in newspaper printing. Like a roll of newsprint, each foil roll will be 6 feet (2 m) wide and 8 miles (12.8 km) long. The printer will deposit a layer of semiconducting ink onto the aluminum. A second press will layer on a necessary chemical like cadmium chloride or zinc oxide. The printed foil will be cut into sheets of solar cells that can be placed between layers of glass or clear plastic and mounted wherever they are needed.

Whereas traditional solar panels cost around three dollars for each watt generated in 2016, a printing process using semiconductor ink could lower that price tenfold, to thirty cents per watt. Printed solar cells are not the stuff of science fiction. In 2017 several companies, including First Solar in Ohio and Honda in Japan, were busy printing out the next-generation solar cells. There are hopes that future cities will be full of homes, businesses, and offices draped with solar cells printed out like newspapers.

thick, about one-third the width of a strand of spiderweb silk. When wavelengths of incoming light are longer than the solar cell is thick, the light is not absorbed.

Biswas and his research team solved the problem with a substance made up of crystalline nanostructures called nanocones. This silicon material has enhanced light-trapping abilities due to the way it is structured. As the name implies, an array of nanocones resemble numerous cone-shaped structures. Under a microscope the nanocones look like pointed bullet tips packed together in a box. The cones have outer coatings of various chemicals, including titanium dioxide and silver. When photons hit the nanocones, wavelengths of red and infrared light are absorbed in a highly efficient manner. If the nanocones were applied to thin-film solar cells currently on the market, they would increase light absorption by up to 15 percent. This increase in efficiency would make the nanocone material competitive with conventional solar cells. As Biswas states, "We were able to design a solar cell with a very thin amount of silicon that could still provide . . . as high [a] performance as the silicon being used today."[23]

Charging Ahead ■

As materials scientists devise new and improved methods for converting the sun's energy to power, solar cell production will require less energy and fewer hazardous chemicals, which will ultimately bring down costs. Next-generation manufacturing techniques will likely put efficient solar cells within financial reach of the general public as producers utilize low-cost printing technology. Printed solar cells might appear on curtains, windows, roof tiles, and other building materials. Advances in thin-film solar could turn cars, clothing, backpacks, and nearly any other surface into an electric generator.

Advances in nanotechnology, quantum physics, and other sciences will make solar cells thinner, lighter, cheaper, and sleeker. These developments make it easy to imagine a future in which today's rooftop solar panels are considered lumbering tech dinosaurs. Science is charging ahead with the goal to provide nearly every electric-powered device with low-cost, efficient energy from the sun.

CHAPTER 4

SOLUTIONS: Building Solar Power Plants

"Without vast amounts of affordable [solar] energy . . . human-driven climate change will result in the eventual destruction of ecosystems and human habitats worldwide."

—John C. Mankins, NASA physicist

Quoted in Diane Stopyra, "Houston, We Have Power: Space-Based Solar Power Could Be the Final Frontier in Renewable Energy," *Salon*, December 4, 2016. www.salon.com.

Many people view solar energy as a do-it-yourself (DIY) technology; individuals decide to take their energy future into their own hands by placing solar panels on their roofs. This DIY spirit will allow solar energy to someday spread out across the land from block to block, until the rooftops of entire cities are filled with solar cells installed by local residents. Although the concept of DIY solar thrives, tech writer Michael Byrne points to a problem with the idea: "Any goofball can plaster their roof with solar panels. . . . That's fine until you run into an unsunny climate or the general real world of already overtaxed humans who just want to pay an electric bill to *whoever* and get on with a restful evening."[24] Byrne's point is that there is a role in the future for large, centralized solar plants that can provide electricity to large numbers of people who do not have the time or money to invest in rooftop solar systems.

Large power plants provide electricity in what is called distributed generation. The plants produce electricity and distribute it over long distances through high-voltage transmission lines. When the term *distributed generation* is applied to solar facilities, it typically refers to plants that generate more than 150 megawatts of electricity when running at full power. According to the utility company Pacific Gas and Electric, that is enough electricity to power about fifty-four thousand homes.

At one time proponents of distributed-generation solar facilities were very optimistic. In 2010 Europe's International Energy Agency predicted that large solar plants would generate nearly one-quarter of the world's electricity by 2050. However, in 2017 distributed-generation solar plants only provided around 2 percent of all solar power generation. Large solar plants faced stiff competition from low-cost electricity produced by natural gas power plants and rooftop solar systems that were getting cheaper every year. Despite the small percentage of electricity provided by distributed-generation solar facilities, scientists and engineers believe that the number of large-scale plants will continue to grow as new systems come online, efficiency rises, and costs come down.

The World's Largest and Cheapest Plant ■

Despite the financial challenges, several enormous solar power plants were under construction in 2017. In Dubai, the world's largest concentrated solar power (CSP) facility was on track to start generating eight hundred megawatts of power by 2020. The plant will contain 2.3 million solar panels and cover 1.8 square miles (4.5 sq. km). Experts predict that when the Dubai plant opens in 2020 it will be the cheapest-operating CSP facility in the world, producing electricity for around eight cents per kilowatt-hour. (In 2017 the cheapest CSP electricity was twelve cents per kilowatt-hour and was produced at the Ouarzazate Solar Power Station in Morocco.) Part of the low cost is due to Dubai's hot desert climate, where the sun shines during nearly 80 percent of the daytime hours. In addition, the facility provides what is referred to as the economics of scale. This means that the building costs are offset by the shear size of the plant, which allows it to produce a greater amount of power than other CSP plants.

The Dubai Electricity and Water Authority (DEWA) plans to keep increasing the size of the CSP facility until it generates a massive five thousand megawatts of power by 2030. This power will provide the nation with 25 percent of its electricity. The design of the Dubai plant is similar to the Ivanpah CSP located in California. Thousands of mirrors concentrate the heat of the sun onto a power tower. Water is pumped through the power tower, where it absorbs the heat of the reflected sunshine. The hot water is then piped to a device called a heat exchanger which creates steam to run electric power turbines.

The DEWA facility will generate twice as much power as Ivan-pah when it opens and about twelve times more power by 2030. Although Dubai is an oil-rich nation, the CSP facility is part of its Clean Energy Strategy, which was enacted to drastically lower the nation's carbon dioxide emissions. As part of the strategy, Dubai planners are hoping to produce 75 percent of the nation's electricity through solar energy by 2075.

Beam-Down Solar Power Technology ■

The DEWA facility relies on proven technology in use at more than sixty CSP power stations throughout the world. Howev-er, these plants are complicated and expensive. In Israel, Abu Dhabi, and Japan, pilot projects known as beam-down power plants utilize a much simpler design, are easier to construct, and take up less land than traditional facilities with their hundreds of thousands of mirrors.

Beam-down power plants rely on an array of thirty ground-based, sun-tracking heliostat mirrors. The light reflected by the heliostats is directed toward an array of forty-five mirrors arranged in concentric circles on the underside of a small tower. The mirrors on the tower beam the con-centrated solar radiation down to a unit that is the heart of the system. It consists of a solar air receiver that is shaped some-thing like a giant metal drinking glass, about 7 feet (2.2 m) in diameter and more than 16 feet (5 m) high. The receiver is integrated with pipes containing thermal storage fluid. The heat that enters the so-lar air receiver heats the fluid to 1,100°F (593°C), producing steam to drive a turbine.

> **WORDS IN CONTEXT**
>
> **concentric**
>
> circles that share the same center, with the larger circle com-pletely surrounding the smaller one

The mirrors on the beam-down tower in Abu Dhabi are mount-ed on a steel frame consisting of three columns that are about 66 feet (20 m) high. Power towers in traditional CSP facilities are much taller, making them more expensive to build and maintain. For example, the tower at Ivanpah is 459 feet (140 m) high, and the world's tallest solar power tower, located in Israel, is 787 feet (240 m) high.

Visitors tour the beam-down solar plant near Abu Dhabi in the United Arab Emirates. Mirrors atop the tower beam concentrated solar radiation to the unit that produces steam, which then drives a turbine.

Beam-down plants also cost less because they eliminate the network of pumps and pipes that transport thermal storage fluid to the top of the power tower. With a beam-down system, the heat transfer and steam generation takes place on the ground beneath the tower. This design allows for faster construction, reduces complexity, and makes maintenance easier.

Floating Solar Facilities

Most solar farms occupy many acres of land, making them impractical in densely populated regions where land prices are high. This factor is motivating some scientists to design and build solar power systems on lakes, bays, marshes, and even ponds where there is plenty of open space. Water-based solar arrays are called floatovoltaics. The panels are specially coated to prevent saltwater corrosion, and they are set on tracking systems that move to maximize sunlight during the course of a day.

Floatovoltaics have several advantages over land-based solar farms. Floatovoltaics lie perfectly flat on the water, and there is no shade to block the sun's rays. The floating panels are more efficient. Ironically, traditional solar panels lose their efficiency as the sun beats down on them and temperatures increase. When solar farms are floating, the water beneath the panels can be used to keep the cells cool. The natural cooling mechanism increases energy output by 8 to 10 percent. And whereas land-based solar farms require constant cleaning in order to maintain efficiency, dust is not a problem on the open water where floatovoltaics are placed. In 2017 floatovoltaics were producing electricity in India, Japan, and Brazil, and projects for floating solar farms were under way in Australia, South Korea, Israel, and elsewhere.

In 2017 only three beam-down CSP facilities were in operation. Scientists are hoping to develop this type of solar power generation for commercial use in small spaces. However, some scientists question the wisdom of beaming solar radiation twice—once from the ground to the main mirrors and a second time to the solar air receiver. These plants have experienced problems when operators had trouble accurately focusing the beamed-down light on the secondary unit. When the light is less concentrated, it loses its power and does not heat as efficiently as a direct beam to a power tower.

Stirling Dish Engines ■

Another CSP system that does not rely on expensive central power towers is based on a technology first conceived by Scottish inventor Robert Stirling in 1816. Stirling invented what is called a heat engine. It consists of two pistons and two cylinders; one of the cylinders in the engine is filled with hydrogen gas. When heat is applied, the hydrogen expands and drives the pistons up and down. When the mechanical power is transferred to a generator, it produces electricity.

In 2015 the Swedish company Ripasso Energy combined the centuries-old Stirling technology with state-of-the-art solar receivers to generate electricity. The system consists of forty precision mirrors mounted on a curved, or parabolic, reflector. The reflector, which is nearly 40 feet (12 m) in diameter, is shaped like a giant satellite dish. The reflector slowly rotates to capture the optimal amount of solar energy. The mirrored surface of the parabolic reflector focuses the sun's energy on a tiny hot point that reaches 1,450°F (788°C). The heat is then applied to the hydrogen in the Stirling engine, which runs rapidly to produce electricity.

The Ripasso dish is highly efficient, meaning it produces electricity at a lower cost than standard CSP systems. The reflector and heat engine convert 34 percent of the sun's energy to grid-ready electricity. Each dish can produce eighty-five megawatt-hours of electricity annually, enough to power twenty-four homes for a year. Additionally, the system does not require water as a thermal storage fluid or to produce steam for a turbine. The minimal water requirements make the system cheap and easy to run in the driest deserts in the world. In fact, the Ripasso pilot project is located in the Kalahari Desert in South Africa. The Kalahari has a climate similar to Arizona, with an average rainfall of 8 inches (20 cm) annually.

The project's site manager in South Africa, Jean-Pierre Fourie, believes Ripasso's system is superior to all others: "What we hope is to become one of the biggest competitors for renewable energy in the world."[25] For this dream to come true, however, Ripasso would have to overcome several shortcomings. Since there is no thermal storage fluid, solar energy cannot be stored for use at night; the reflectors only work with consistent, bright sunshine. And if the technology was put to work in a large commercial system, the company would have to build a solar farm with thousands of reflectors and Stirling engines in one place. A nine-hundred-megawatt solar plant would require thirty-six thousand identical dishes. Each reflector requires a separate engine, and each engine needs regular maintenance and repair. These maintenance requirements would create very high labor costs for a solar farm with tens of thousands of heat engines. Despite the drawbacks, Ripasso was working to finance its first large commercial solar farm in 2017.

Linear Fresnel Reflectors ■

Most CSP facilities are built on a vertical scale, with dishes and towers rising high into the air. But the cheapest large-scale solar prototype is a horizontal system; it is long and runs parallel to the ground. The compact linear Fresnel reflector (CLFR) consists of long mirrors mounted side by side in a parabolic trough. The mirrors are set at a specific angle to increase the intensity of the solar energy by 30 percent. The sunlight is concentrated on elevated receivers, called absorbers. These consist of a system of boiler tubes, filled with water, and located above the mirrors. The concentrated sunlight raises the water temperature between 750°F and 900°F (400°C and 482°C). The high temperatures create superheated steam that is used to spin turbines and generate electricity.

WORDS IN CONTEXT

absorber

a system of boiler tubes filled with water, located above the mirrors on some types of solar power facilities

There are numerous factors that make CLFR systems cheaper than other CSP facilities. The flat mirrors are much less expensive to manufacture than the highly engineered parabolic reflectors used in conventional solar plants. Unlike facilities with power towers, the mirrors are not motorized to follow the movements of the sun, which makes them cheaper to maintain. The ground-based CLFR system does not have to be reinforced like large parabolic dishes and can withstand strong winds that are a constant factor in the desert environment. Likewise, the system requires less land area; proponents claim a CLFR can generate one and a half to three times more power from a square mile of desert than a power tower system.

Concentrated solar power (CSP) facilities utilize large mirrors to capture sunlight and heat a fluid that is used to power a turbine that generates electricity. The CSP system known as the compact linear Fresnel reflector (CLFR) employs flat or slightly curved mirrors placed in rows that run parallel to the ground. A liquid-filled receiver is placed above the mirrors. When sunlight hits the mirrors, the solar energy is reflected onto the receiver, which heats the liquid to more than 750°F (400°C). The superheated liquid is used to spin a turbine that generates electricity.

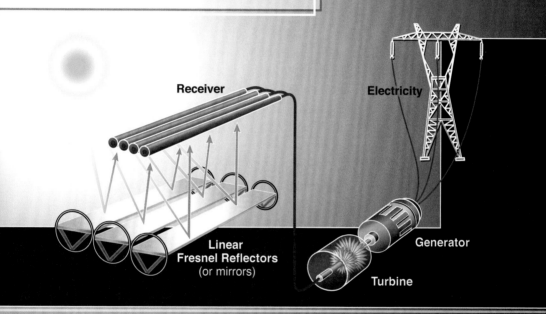

Receiver

Electricity

Linear
Fresnel Reflectors
(or mirrors)

Generator

Turbine

Source: Office of Energy Efficiency & Renewable Energy, "Linear Concentrator System Basics for Concentrating Solar Power." August 20, 2013. https://energy.gov.

Three facilities, located in Australia, Jordan, and Bakersfield, California, use CLFR technology. The Kimberlina Solar Thermal Energy Plant in Bakersfield generates five megawatts of power from thirteen CLFR collectors. The facility, completed in 2011, has a small footprint; it occupies 12.7 acres (1.1 ha) of desert. The plant also produces excess steam, which is used to boost performance at a nearby natural gas power plant. Despite the success of the plant, there are few companies rushing to build CLFR facilities. The solar thermal industry has long been dominated by systems dependent on parabolic mirrors, and few investors seem willing to take a chance on CLFR technology because it has not yet been tested in a wide variety of circumstances.

Space-Based Solar Power ■

CSP systems can beam sunlight up, down, and sideways and utilize curved dishes, flat mirrors, power towers, and heat engines. But there are limits to every system; they are inefficient under cloudy skies, and some stop producing power as the sun sinks below the horizon. These unavoidable facts have some scientists looking to a place where the sun always shines—outer space.

Researchers at NASA have been working on ways to build space-based solar power stations since the 1960s. The designs feature huge arrays of solar panels placed in what is called geosynchronous orbit, a spot 22,236 miles (35,785 km) above Earth's equator. There are numerous advantages to space-based solar power stations. They can deliver up to forty times more energy than a system of similar size located on the ground. Clouds, water vapor, dust, and dim winter sun do not exist in space, and it is never nighttime. Orbiting solar energy systems would be able to intercept sun rays that are 35 to 70 percent more intense than those on the ground. Such a system could produce power twenty-four hours a day, which means there would be no need to store power in large batteries or other devices for nighttime use.

The Japan Aerospace Exploration Agency (JAXA) is working on a space-based solar power design that features huge, ultrathin mirrors that would stretch 2.1 miles (3.5 km) across space. The mirrors are lightweight and are made with a synthetic polymer-based resin that is exceptionally strong and highly resistant to the heat and radiation of outer space. The mirrors are specially designed to absorb a broad range of the electromagnetic spectrum, making maximum use of sunlight by reflecting 95 percent of the total energy.

The mirrors would absorb sunlight from almost any angle and redirect it onto a smaller photovoltaic receptor. The power would be converted to laser or microwave energy and beamed down to Earth. It would be received by a large station on the ground that would collect the energy, convert it to AC electricity, and feed it into the grid. The energy, whether from a microwave or laser, would only be as intense as the midday sun, so birds or airplanes flying through the beam would be safe. However, assembling the JAXA facility would be very complicated; numerous rocket launches would be required to carry the mirrors into space and the power station would have to be assembled by astronauts.

The US military has been researching space-based solar power because it is portable; an army unit on the move could operate a semitruck with a power receiver mounted on a trailer. When power was needed in the field, scientists at NASA could focus the energy on the receiver, instantly providing electricity for

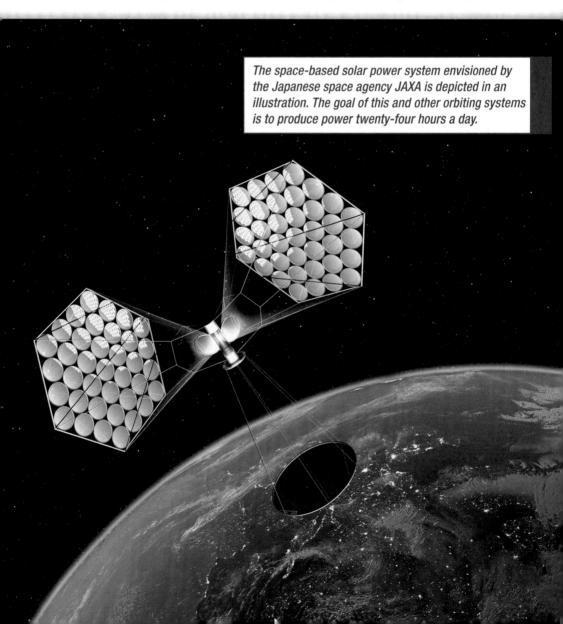

The space-based solar power system envisioned by the Japanese space agency JAXA is depicted in an illustration. The goal of this and other orbiting systems is to produce power twenty-four hours a day.

all of the unit's needs. This system could also be put to work in disaster areas.

The idea of dozens of space-based solar power stations supplying much of the world's demand for electricity might sound like science fiction. But Japan envisions building a space-based station by 2040, and China, the world's largest energy consumer, has plans to have its first space-based system operational by 2050. Like the nation itself, China's plans are big: its station would be 2.6 square miles (6.7 sq. km), about twice the size of New York City's Central Park. It would weigh 10,000 tons (9,073 t), making it larger than anything ever put into space.

Not everyone agrees that space-based solar power should be deployed. In 2012 Elon Musk said the US government should "stab that thing in the heart"[26] because of the $10 billion estimated cost of building a massive solar power station in space. However,

Moon-Based Solar Power

The moon is a giant solar collector; solar radiation constantly illuminates its surface with 13,000 terawatts of power, or one thousand times more than humanity uses in a year. Houston physicist David Criswell has dreamed of harvesting the moon's solar power since 1975. Criswell envisions a lunar-based solar power (LSP) system consisting of ten 62-mile-wide (100 km) circular solar collectors placed on the light side of the moon, which faces Earth at all times. The energy would be converted to microwaves that would be beamed to hundreds of receivers on Earth. Criswell is convinced that an LSP system delivering 0.1 terawatts of electric power could be constructed within a ten-year timeframe, and within forty years the facility could supply 20 terawatts of electricity. Criswell believes that an LSP system needs to be built as soon as possible: "By the year 2050, ten billion people will require at least 2 kilowatts of electricity per person or a global total of 20 terawatts. . . . I really think the Moon is our only option for sustainable and affordable electric power on a global scale."

Quoted in Bruce Dorminey, "Physicist Wants to Beam Solar Energy Back from Moon's Surface," *Forbes*, March 28, 2017. www.forbes.com.

space-based solar power proponents point out that costly systems would be worthwhile because they would address concerns about a growing energy-hungry population, climate change, and other needs. As spacecraft engineer Paul Jaffe points out, cheap, abundant solar power is needed in developing countries to fight "poverty, water scarcity, poor health, lack of education and political instability."[27]

"Growing at Warp Speed" ■

In 2016 solar power was the number-one source of all new electric generation added to the grid in the United States. Led by large-scale utility providers, 16 gigawatts of solar were delivered to the grid, more than doubling the record-breaking 7.3 gigawatts of 2015. Distributed-generation solar was experiencing similar growth in Europe, China, India, and elsewhere. As Tom Kimbis of the trade group Solar Energy Industries Association points out, "The solar industry is growing at warp speed, driven by the fact that solar is one of the lowest-cost options for electricity."[28] There are still problems with the profitability of large-scale solar facilities, but researchers, scientists, and engineers continue to search for cheaper, simpler, and more efficient ways to generate grid-scale solar power. While thousands continue to plaster their rooftops with solar panels, new large-scale systems are being designed and implemented from California to the Kalahari. And with plans for space-based systems, the sky will no longer be the limit when it comes to producing solar power.

CHAPTER 5

SOLUTIONS:
Solar Energy Storage

"[Solar] energy storage is an emissions-free capacity resource that is fast, highly flexible, and always on and ready to . . . deliver or withdraw power from the grid depending on what is needed and when it's most valuable."

—Brian Perusse, director of AES Energy Storage

Quoted in Kyle Rabin, "Greening the Grid: Utility-Scale Energy Storage," *Huffington Post*, January 13, 2012. www.huffingtonpost.com.

Germany sometimes has a power generation problem that is seen as highly ironic—on some days the nation produces too much solar power. At one point in May 2016, over 90 percent of Germany's power was coming from renewable energy. Although this seems like great news for the environment, Germany does not have a good way to store the excess solar power generated. Coal power plants are kept idling. These fossil fuel plants cannot easily ramp down in response to excess solar supplies on the power grid; if they are shut off, it can take four to eight hours to get them running again. When the sun goes down, the coal plants get fired up.

Around 40 percent of German electricity is produced by coal. But in an effort to slow climate change, Germany passed laws to reduce carbon dioxide emissions 40 percent below 1990 levels by 2020 and 80 percent below those levels by 2050. If Germany is to meet this ambitious goal, it needs to rapidly develop large-scale solar energy storage facilities. And this is true wherever utilities are generating excess solar energy on bright, sunny days. That is why scientists and engineers are working every day to develop new storage systems for solar power with efforts aimed at increasing efficiency and driving down costs.

A Pumped-Storage Battery ■

Germany is moving beyond coal—and creating a new way to store solar energy—by converting an old coal mine into a solar storage battery. Prosper-Haniel, a coal mine located in the German state of North Rhine–Westphalia, will store power using twentieth-century technology with a modern twist. When operational in 2018, the mine will operate like a hydroelectric power plant, which produces electricity through mechanical energy. Hydroelectric plants store water in a reservoir behind a dam. When the water is released, it cascades downward to spin a large turbine that generates electricity. After the water passes through the turbines, it is carried away by a river located beneath the dam at a lower elevation.

The system planned for the German coal mine is called pumped storage. Like a hydroelectric dam, it will have a surface reservoir where water is stored; the released water will spin electric turbines located near the top of the mine. But the water will not flow away in a river. Instead, it will be captured in more than 16 miles (25.7 km) of mine shafts, some located 4,000 feet (1,200 m) beneath the earth's surface. The water will remain underground until excess solar power is being added to the nation's grid on sunny days. Operators can then use the excess electricity to run giant electric pumps that will move the water back to the surface reservoir.

There are a few pumped-storage facilities in the United States and elsewhere, but the German project is the first to repurpose a coal mine for renewable energy use. The facility will produce two hundred megawatts of hydroelectric power, enough to power more than four hundred thousand homes. Brian Parkin, a journalist who specializes in energy issues, explains the advantages of converting a nineteenth-century power source into a twenty-first-century energy generator:

> Germany's decision to turn a coal mine into a pumped-hydro-storage station may solve two of the most intractable challenges created by its shift to clean power. On a local level, it provides new economic activity in a region where generations of workers have relied on fossil fuel for their livelihoods. On a regional level, it catalyzes the expansion of renewable energy by helping to maintain electric capacity even when the wind doesn't blow or the sun doesn't shine.[29]

Soaking Up Excess Solar Power ■

Like Germany, California is also trying to reduce CO_2 emissions 80 percent by 2050. But the state has the same problem; at times large-scale solar facilities are adding more power to the grid than Californians can use. However, as Nancy Traweek, the director of California's grid operations, points out, solar is not dependable: "All of a sudden you have a major cloud that comes over a solar field . . . that causes the solar power to drop off. That [power] needs to come from somewhere else immediately."[30] The power often comes from natural gas plants known as peakers, which can be turned on quickly when demand for electricity peaks.

Natural gas utilities emit half the amount of CO_2 as coal plants, but peaker plants are still at odds with California's goal to reduce carbon emissions. Engineers and scientists are working to replace some of the state's peakers with massive solar storage sites consisting of lithium-ion batteries. The facilities will be powered by oversized versions of the batteries found in laptops, smartphones, and other common digital devices.

In 2017 the AES Corporation was building three energy storage sites in Southern California. AES spent nine years working with manufacturers of electric-car batteries to learn how to assemble and control ever-bigger constellations of lithium-ion batteries. The facility under construction in Escondido, located 30 miles (48 km) north of San Diego, was expected to be the largest in the world. From the street, the 1.5 acre (0.6 ha) site owned by San Diego Gas & Electric (SDG&E), seems unremarkable. Once completed, it was to include twenty-four beige steel shipping containers, similar to the steel boxes on trailers pulled by big eighteen-wheeler trucks. But inside the containers, engineers were assembling a high-tech, cutting-edge solar storage system. The containers could hold nineteen thousand lithium-ion battery modules that can store thirty megawatts of electricity. Each module is the size of a kitchen drawer, and they were being wired together in racks.

The SDG&E facility will do something that has never been done, as energy journalists Diane Cardwell and Clifford Krauss explain: "[The batteries] will serve as a kind of sponge, soaking up excess or low-cost solar energy during the day and then squeezing it back into the grid in the evening, when demand surges as the sun sets. There is enough capacity in the containers full of batteries to power about 20,000 homes for four hours."[31] The electricity from the batteries will be cheaper and more flexible than peaker power and better for the environment. AES is planning an even larger installation in Long Beach, California, due to go online in 2020. The $1 billion battery storage facility, slated to replace an aging peaker plant, will store one hundred megawatts of power. When completed, the Long Beach facility will have eighteen thousand battery modules, each the size of a compact car.

The AES battery storage arrays in Escondido, California, are pictured. This facility will gather excess solar power during the day and move it back into the power grid when demand surges at night.

AES is taking advantage of the push by power companies throughout the world to build bigger and better solar storage facilities. A company project in Morgan, Australia, called the Riverland Solar Storage facility, is scheduled to go online in 2019. This plant will combine the world's largest solar farm with a huge onsite battery storage facility. Riverland will feature 3.4 million solar cells generating 330 megawatts of power. Excess electricity will flow into 1.1 million lithium-ion batteries storing a total of 100 megawatts of power.

The AES projects use batteries manufactured by the South Korean electronics giant Samsung, a company familiar with the dangers associated with lithium-ion batteries. Samsung was forced to recall 2.5 million of the company's Galaxy Note 7 smartphones in October 2016 after nearly a hundred phones exploded into flames. The problem was due to a design flaw with the lithium-ion batteries that power the phone. AES engineers believe they have eliminated the risk of battery fires at solar storage facilities. The containers holding the batteries are temperature controlled, and the battery packs are outfitted with advanced monitoring and ventilation equipment. However, like all lithium-ion batteries, the massive storage batteries will need to be replaced as they wear out over time.

Anodes and Nanotubes ■

Researchers are working to create safer, longer-lasting, and more powerful batteries by improving the electrochemical reactions between cathodes, anodes, electrolytes, and other battery elements. One way scientists are hoping to improve anodes is by reducing or eliminating graphite. The lithium-ion batteries that power a typical electric car like a Tesla contain 110 pounds (50 kg) of graphite, but batteries in a large-scale storage facility like the one in Long Beach will use tons of graphite.

Graphite is a form of carbon used as "lead" in pencils. Graphite mining, which mostly occurs in China, is associated with serious pollution problems. Additionally, lithium-ion batteries can only be made with graphite that is 99.9 percent pure. The process for creating graphite of this purity is expensive and wasteful. These reasons are why scientists at Nanyang Technology University (NTU) in Singapore are researching ways to replace graphite

Rocks, Trains, and Mechanical Power

Mechanical energy storage is most often associated with dams and hydroelectric power plants. But there are other ways to store energy in a mechanical device. In 2016 an energy company called Advanced Rail Energy Storage (ARES) began work on a mechanical energy storage system in Pahrump, Nevada. The $55 million system consists of a 5.5-mile (9 km) railroad track and 9,600 tons (8,709 t) of rock filling a few railcars. The track runs 3,000 feet (914 m) up the side of a mountain. The railcars, built with twentieth-century technology, are the type used to haul ore from mining operations. In a twenty-first-century twist, the wheels of the railcars are outfitted with electric generators. When the local utility has excess solar power during the day, ARES uses the energy to run the train up the mountain. When the utility needs the power at sunset, the train rolls slowly down the mountain and the generators in the wheels produce electricity that is then funneled into the grid.

When the Pahrump project is completed in 2019, it will be able to store about fifty megawatts of energy. The technology could also be expanded into larger systems. Additionally, the rail system uses existing technology, is easy to operate, and is much cheaper to build than a hydroelectric dam. As Francesca Cava, the vice president of operations at ARES, says, "We don't have to wait until the next big scientific discovery to solve the storage problem. It will work for a long time, and it's cost effective."

Quoted in Patrick J. Kiger, "A Train That Goes Nowhere Could Change How We Store Energy," ARES, June 10, 2016. www.aresnorthamerica.com.

anodes with titanium dioxide nanotubes. Titanium dioxide is a safe, abundant chemical found in soil. It is commonly used in sunscreen lotions. When converted to nanotubes, titanium dioxide molecules make excellent conductors of electricity. The nanotubes can withstand high temperatures and are incredibly strong for their tiny size and weight.

Titanium dioxide nanotubes speed up chemical reactions in the electrolyte of batteries, which allows for superfast charging. A titanium dioxide battery can be fully charged in about twelve minutes.

This type of battery would greatly benefit consumers with rooftop solar systems. Lithium-ion storage batteries like the Powerwall take up to four hours to charge. A nanotube battery would quickly recharge even on days when the sun was intermittent. Titanium dioxide batteries also have a much longer life; they can endure ten thousand charging cycles—or every day for twenty-seven years. The large lithium-ion battery packs being installed by SDG&E and other utilities are only expected to last around five years.

In 2016 an Israeli company called UltraCharge Limited established a pilot facility to manufacture titanium dioxide nanotube anodes based on the NTU research. UltraCharge was working with storage battery users across a range of industries to provide the anode material for testing. The ultimate goal of the company is to produce efficient energy storage systems for the alternative energy industry.

Bio-Inspired Energy ■

While some researchers work to improve anodes, a team of Australian scientists at RMIT University in Melbourne found a unique method to make electrodes work better. Researchers say the design idea was bio-inspired—based on the biology of a plant. The scientists were searching for a way to create an electrode with nanotubes. They were inspired by nature's solution for efficiently circulating water through a plant called the western sword fern. The plant contains intricate self-repeating geometric patterns called fractals. As lead scientist Min Gu explains, "The leaves of the western sword fern are densely crammed with veins, making them extremely efficient for storing energy and transporting water around the plant. . . . Our electrode is based on these fractal shapes—which are self-replicating, like the mini structures within snowflakes—and we've used this naturally-efficient design to improve solar energy storage at a nano level."[32]

Using the fern's natural fractal design, researchers packed millions of electricity-storing nanotubes onto an extremely small

The western sword fern (pictured) efficiently stores energy and circulates water through its leaves and stems. Scientists in Australia are working on an electrode that was inspired by this plant.

electrode. The electrode is designed to work with batteries known as supercapacitors, or supercaps, that hold three hundred times more power than lithium-ion batteries. Supercaps can be charged instantly and suffer very little degradation over time. Australian researchers believe they can integrate the tiny electrodes directly into thin-film solar cells. In 2017 this work was in the experimental stages. If tests are successful, the researchers will be able to create a material with the ability to both harvest and store the energy of the sun, eliminating the need to build expensive, large-scale storage facilities.

Rust Power ■

The goal of creating solar cells that can store their own power is leading scientists at Stanford University to examine rust, a substance most people would rather do without. Rust is generally thought of as a destructive force that corrodes cars, machinery, and tools. But scientists have found a new use for rust that might allow for the creation of solar panels that generate electricity that can be used when the sun is not shining.

The chemical name for rust is iron oxide. It is one of three metal oxides, along with bismuth vanadium oxide and titanium oxide, that can be formed into solar cells. Scientists have long known the solar potential of metal oxides. However, metal oxide solar cells are less efficient than silicon cells when converting photons to electrons. The Stanford team discovered that heat can make metal oxide cells much more efficient. In contrast, silicon solar cells lose efficiency under high temperatures. Metal oxide solar cells produce more electrons when the solar heat is concentrated on the surface of the cell using a magnifying lens or parabolic mirror. Stanford materials science professor William Chueh explains

Iron oxide, the chemical name for rust, is one of three metal oxides that can be used to create solar cells. Scientists are researching ways to use this cheap, plentiful, easy-to-use source for making more efficient and cost-effective solar cells.

the finding: "We've shown that inexpensive, abundant and readily processed metal oxides could become better producers of electricity than was previously supposed."[33]

The excess electricity produced by the metal oxide solar cell can be used to separate water into its basic elements, hydrogen and oxygen. Water, or H_2O, contains two hydrogen atoms and one oxygen atom. Although it is a major component of water, hydrogen by itself is extremely flammable. Hydrogen burns clean—it does not produce CO_2—and creates three times as much energy as a similar amount of natural gas. Hydrogen is separated from water through a technique called electrolysis, which uses DC electricity to split the hydrogen molecules off from the oxygen molecules.

The high temperatures generated by metal oxide solar cells doubled the rate of hydrogen production during electrolysis when compared to silicon cells. The pure hydrogen gas created through solar electrolysis is a form of chemical energy storage. Hydrogen can be used to power fuel cells. These high-tech batteries convert the chemical energy of hydrogen into electricity and can be used in homes to provide power when solar panels are not producing energy. Fuel cells are also used to power cars like the Toyota Mirai and the Honda Clarity.

Researchers believe that this discovery will encourage solar cell manufacturers to develop metal oxide cells with built-in hydrogen production abilities. As Chueh explains, "We can store these gases, we can transport them through pipelines, and when we burn them we don't release any extra carbon. It's a carbon-neutral energy cycle."[34]

Heat and Molecules ■

Although solar-generated heat can be stored as hydrogen gas, researchers in Sweden are experimenting with ways to store thermal energy in a liquid form as well. Chemists at Chalmers University of Technology are conducting research into molecules called isomers. An isomer is a molecule with the same molecular formula as a conventional chemical but with a different chemical structure or arrangement of atoms. The varied structure gives the isomer different properties than the original chemical.

> **WORDS IN CONTEXT**
>
> **isomer**
>
> a molecular variation of a compound with the same formula as the original compound but with a different arrangement of atoms, which gives it different properties

Thermal Energy Storage with Molten Salt

When the Crescent Dunes Solar Energy plant near Tonopah, Nevada, began operating in 2016, it was the first utility-scale facility in the world to feature molten salt energy storage capabilities. The facility features a complex network of pipes that circulates 5,800 gallons (21,955 L) of molten salt every minute through a 640-foot (195 m) power tower. Ten thousand solar reflecting heliostats heat the molten salt to 1,050°F (566°C). The heated liquid is used to produce steam to power electric turbines. After the sun goes down, the molten salt cools to 500°F but remains hot enough to provide power to seventy-five thousand Nevada homes for ten hours. Molten salt can stay hot for months, and it is cycled daily, replenished by the sun, and used during peak demand periods.

The molten salt storage system at the Crescent Dunes facility can store the equivalent of one gigawatt of power. This amount is more than twice the capabilities of the largest battery storage systems. And the plant operates at a very low cost when compared to other solar storage methods. The US Department of Energy estimated that battery prices were about $125 per kilowatt-hour in 2017. That is more than four times the cost, per kilowatt-hour, of the thermal energy stored by the Crescent Dunes molten salt system. And whereas batteries last five to ten years, the system at Crescent Dunes is projected to provide reliable, emissions-free electricity to consumers for more than thirty years.

When searching for a chemical that would be useful for thermal energy storage, researchers created an isomer with double bonds. Most molecules have single bonds, meaning they are held together by two bonding electrons. An isomer with a double bond is held together by four bonding electrons. When the isomer is exposed to solar energy, the double bond breaks as it absorbs the heat, creating a single bond between the molecules. When scientists add various chemicals, called catalysts, the process is reversed. Single bonds return to their previous state as double bonds. During this reversal process, the stored thermal energy is released.

In 2017 the isomers created by the Swedish chemists could only store low amounts of heat energy. But they believe they can create isomers that can store a great deal of heat, up to several hundred degrees. The chemists are hoping to invent a system filled with a chemical liquid that will absorb sunlight in an efficient way and release it as heat to generate electricity at night or during cloudy weather. The molecular thermal system will work in tandem with rooftop solar systems, creating a universal solar energy battery that releases heat on demand.

Unpredictable Power ■

Solar energy can be stored in isomers, lithium-ion batteries, nanotubes, hydrogen, molten salt, pumped water, and numerous other systems. Although each of these methods holds promise, none has been perfected. As such, solar power remains an unpredictable resource, subject to the whims of weather and the unchanging rotation of the earth around the sun. But chemists, biologists, engineers, mathematicians, and technicians in nearly every branch of science are rising to the challenges presented by that endless source of energy that radiates from the sky. They hope to usher in a future in which the heat and light of the sun provides a steady, efficient, and predictable source of power every day and night throughout the year.

> **WORDS IN CONTEXT**
>
> **molten**
>
> liquefied by heat

SOURCE NOTES

CHAPTER 1
CURRENT STATUS: Sunlight to Electricity

1. Quoted in Alan Chodos, "April 25, 1954: Bell Labs Demonstrates the First Practical Silicon Solar Cell," *American Physical Society News*, April 2009. www.aps.org.
2. Jennifer Robison, "Rooftop Solar Power Grows Despite Waning Incentives," *Las Vegas Review-Journal,* March 21, 2015. www.reviewjournal.com.
3. Quoted in Zachary Shahan, "5 Elon Musk Interviews, Tons of Awesome Quotes," Clean Technica, December 21, 2014. http://cleantechnica.com.

CHAPTER 2
PROBLEMS: Efficiency and Cost

4. Quoted in Sarah Rieger, "Solar Power Will Soon Be Cheaper than Coal," *Huffington Post*, January 4, 2017. www.huffingtonpost.ca.
5. Quoted in Mark Shwartz, "New Technology Makes Metal Wires on Solar Cells Nearly Invisible to Light," Phys.org, November 25, 2015. https://phys.org.
6. Quoted in Sarah Zhang, "A Huge Solar Plant Caught Fire, and That's the Least of Its Problems," *Wired*, May 23, 2016. www.wired.com.
7. Richard Martin, "Ivanpah's Problems Could Signal the End of Concentrated Solar in the U.S.," *MIT Technology Review*, March 24, 2016. www.technologyreview.com.
8. Quoted in Karl Mathiesen, "What Is Holding Back the Growth of Solar Power," *Guardian*, January 21, 2016. www.theguardian.com.
9. Quoted in Richard Martin, "Germany Runs Up Against the Limits of Renewables," *MIT Technology Review,* May 24, 2016. www.technologyreview.com.

10. Seth Blumsack, "Why Rooftop Solar Is Disruptive to Utilities—and the Grid," *Conversation*, March 24, 2015. http://thecon versation.com.

11. Quoted in Chris Taylor, "Elon Musk Unveils Tesla Powerwall Batteries to 'Change the World,'" *Mashable*, April 30, 2015. http://mashable.com.

12. Zhang, "A Huge Solar Plant Caught Fire, and That's the Least of Its Problems."

13. Quoted in Russ Mitchell, "An Auto Legend's Blunt Take on Tesla and Trump," *Los Angeles Times,* March 31, 2017, p. C7.

CHAPTER 3
SOLUTIONS: Improving Solar Cells

14. Quoted in Yngve Vogt, "Nano Tricks Boost Solar Cell Efficiency," *Controlled Environments*, March 27, 2017. www.cemag.us.

15. Quoted in Vogt, "Nano Tricks Boost Solar Cell Efficiency."

16. Robert F. Service, "Low-Cost Solar Cells Poised for Commercial Breakthrough," *Science*, December 7, 2016. www.sciencemag.org.

17. Quoted in Kathryn Nave, "The Simple, Cheap Trick That Makes Solar Panels More Efficient," *Wired*, August 30, 2016. www.wired.co.uk.

18. Quoted in David L. Chandler, "Hot New Solar Cell," MIT News, May 23, 2016. http://news.mit.edu.

19. Quoted in Kyle Jaeger, "How the World's Blackest Material Could Improve Solar Energy," ATTN:, March 31, 2017. www.attn.com.

20. Quoted in Phys.org, "Quantum Dot Solar Windows Go Nontoxic, Colorless, with Record Efficiency," August 25, 2015. https://phys.org.

21. Tina Casey, "A First for Perovskite Solar Cells: Quantum Dots & 'Exceptional' Efficiency," Clean Technica, October 11, 2016. https://cleantechnica.com.

22. Quoted in Kathy Kincade, "Working Towards Super-Efficient, Ultra-Thin Silicon Solar Cells," Phys.org, March 21, 2017. https://phys.org.

23. Quoted in Kincade, "Working Towards Super-Efficient, Ultra-Thin Silicon Solar Cells."

CHAPTER 4
SOLUTIONS: Building Solar Power Plants

24. Michael Byrne, "The Solar Future May Still Hinge on Old-School Centralized Power Generation," Motherboard, June 22, 2014. https://motherboard.vice.com.
25. Quoted in Jeffrey Barbee, "Could This Be the World's Most Efficient Solar Electricity System?," *Guardian*, May 13, 2015. www.theguardian.com.
26. Quoted in Diane Stopyra, "Houston, We Have Power: Space-Based Solar Power Could Be the Final Frontier in Renewable Energy," Salon, December 4, 2016. www.salon.com.
27. Quoted in Stopyra, "Houston, We Have Power."
28. Quoted in Chris Martin, "Solar Makes Up Most of the New U.S. Power Capacity for First Time," Bloomberg, June 8, 2016. www.bloomberg.com.

CHAPTER 5
SOLUTIONS: Solar Energy Storage

29. Brian Parkin, "How to Make Electricity in a Disused Coal Mine," Bloomberg, March 16, 2017. www.bloomberg.com.
30. Quoted in Lauren Sommer, "What Will California Do with Too Much Solar?," KQED, April 4, 2016. ww2.kqed.org.
31. Diane Cardwell and Clifford Krauss, "A Big Test for Big Batteries," *New York Times*, January 14, 2017. www.nytimes.com.
32. Quoted in RMIT University, "Bio-Inspired Energy Storage," ScienceDaily, March 31, 2017. www.sciencedaily.com.
33. Quoted in Glen Martin, "Stanford Engineers Use Rust to Build a Solar-Powered Battery," Stanford News, February 25, 2016. http://news.stanford.edu.
34. Quoted in Martin, "Stanford Engineers Use Rust to Build a Solar-Powered Battery."

Books

John Allen, *What Is the Future of Nanotechnology?* San Diego: ReferencePoint, 2016.

Anne Cunningham, *Critical Perspectives on Fossil Fuels vs. Renewable Energy*. New York: Enslow, 2017.

Sylvia Engdahl, *Alternative Energy.* Farmington Hills, MI: Greenhaven, 2015.

Robert Green, *How Renewable Energy Is Changing Society.* San Diego: ReferencePoint, 2015.

Audrey Huggett, *Solar Energy Projects.* Seattle: Cherry Lake, 2016.

Websites

Clean Technica (https://cleantechnica.com). This popular website focuses on solar and wind power, clean transportation, energy efficiency, and clean energy storage. Features include articles and videos about clean energy, environmental news, electric car reviews, and information about household solar and wind systems.

E&E News (www.eenews.net). This website covers current events of interest to the general public and to energy and environmental professionals. It contains sections like Energywire, Greenwire, and Climatewire dedicated to keeping up with the latest environmental news.

Green Tech Media (www.greentechmedia.com). Dedicated to emerging green and clean technologies, this site provides news, information about projects, and research into alternative energy sources.

International Energy Agency (www.iea.org). This organization works with twenty-nine member countries to focus on energy security, economic development, and environmental awareness. The website contains comprehensive information about solar energy, the smart grid, carbon capture, efficiency, renewables, climate change, and other issues.

National Nanotechnology Initiative (www.nano.gov). The National Nanotechnology Initiative is a US government research and development initiative aimed at understanding and controlling matter at the nanoscale level. The website features current events, describes the importance of nanotechnology, and features a link to the educational site Nanotechnology 101.

Internet Sources

Reja Amatya et al., "The Future of Solar Energy," MIT Energy Initiative, 2015. http://energy.mit.edu/wp-content/uploads/2015/05 /MITEI-The-Future-of-Solar-Energy.pdf.

Solar Reserve, "Crescent Dunes," 2017. www.solarreserve.com /en/global-projects/csp/crescent-dunes.

Diane Stopyra, "Houston, We Have Power: Space-Based Solar Power Could Be the Final Frontier in Renewable Energy," Salon, December 4, 2016. www.salon.com/2016/12/04/houston-we -have-power-space-based-solar-power-could-be-the-final-frontier -in-renewable-energy.

INDEX

78

ABOUT THE AUTHOR

Stuart A. Kallen is the author of more than 350 nonfiction books for children and young adults. He has written on topics ranging from the theory of relativity to the art of electronic dance music. In addition, Kallen has written award-winning children's videos and television scripts. In his spare time he is a singer, songwriter, and guitarist in San Diego.